ADAM

Lord Loveday Ememe

By Lord Loveday Ememe and available from Lulu and Amazon.
The constitution and policing
Heresy
Starfleet
The Supernatural
Creation
Deterrence
Stalking
The media

www.lulu.com
Copyright© Lord Loveday Ememe 2013
The author asserts the moral right to be recognized as the author of this work.
ISBN: 978-1-291-36832-1

ADAM

Table of Contents

1. A jury of your peers
2. A blame the victim culture by the uncivilized
3. The ultimate miscarriage of justice
4. Author's notes
5. Author's biography
6. Bibliography

1. A jury of your peers

ADAM

According to the constitution, the bible, Lord Adam was created in the Garden of Eden. He was also created civilized without supernatural powers and senses. He was created to be ruler or system lord or law lord. The civilized constitution is a living representation of the law unlike the uncivilized constitution that is political by nature.

The political uncivilized constitution is similar to an undeveloped foetus without form. The uncivilized have demonstrated an inability to have a truthful well-formed conversation with the civilized their rulers. The uncivilized political constitution is not compatible with the civilized constitution. It is impossible and extremely unhealthy for the civilized when the uncivilized want to establish a political supernatural relationship with the civilized. It is beyond the natural capabilities of the civilized constitution. Such relationships are one sided and dictatorial and subject to supernatural manipulations by the uncivilized. Domestic and international laws do not recognize the uncivilized constitution as human beings especially with regard to contact with the recognized constitution, the civilized constitution. This will suggest that these laws consider it unsafe and unlawful for the uncivilized to have contact with the civilized whether they pretend to be civilized or not.

The uncivilized interact with each other by role playing or acting or pretending to the point of self-destruction, which is unsafe for the civilized. The rules governing acting or role play requires all parties involved to consent beforehand and to know beforehand what will happen similar to a movie script and it must be safe for the parties involved. This is compatible with the supernatural constitution but beyond the natural capabilities of the civilized constitution. This is why some of the supernatural social activities have extremely unhealthy effects on the civilized. The uncivilized prepare mentally beforehand.

The uncivilized are political by nature and the civilized are not and the uncivilized are not allowed to expose or involve the civilized directly or indirectly in their political supernatural activities. The systems of government in Japan and the United Kingdom have the separation of powers doctrine in place, the political classes and the ruler (monarch) and the nobility. The ruler is meant to be of a civilized constitution without supernatural powers and senses and the political classes are meant to be the uncivilized with supernatural powers and senses. The civil constitution is severely mentally impaired of intelligence for political supernatural lawless activities, whether the uncivilized pretend to be civilized or not during these activities.

It is safe to conclude that the civilized and the uncivilized are different species and belong to different peer groups. In the criminal justice system, a suspect in a crime can only be judge by his or her peer group, you can only be judged by a jury of your peers. In most social activities or in most situations in life requiring interactions with other people in an official capability or personal situations a degree of judgement is required. This is why all legislations in the United Kingdom only authorizes interactions or contacts between the civilized and not the uncivilized whether the uncivilized pretend to be civilized or not.

When a civilized person without supernatural powers and senses is surrounded by the uncivilized with supernatural powers and senses, the civilized person is famous, a natural star, with all the problems famous people experience without the necessary protection from unwanted approaches by the uncivilized. The life of the civilized person will always revolve around supernatural manipulations by the uncivilized to use the celebrity of the civilized person for things similar to the endorsements of products or activities without any benefits to the civilized person. The supernatural manipulations include exploiting the needs of the civilized to force unhealthy unnecessary unlawful contact. The supernatural manipulations also include situations where the uncivilized are unlawfully ruling instead of the civilized. It also involves the unlawful use of the civilized as test subjects for the blue, red and orange political supernatural activities. These political supernatural activities are beyond the natural capabilities of the civilized constitution to cope with because of the harmful effects of supernaturalism on the civil constitution, direct or indirect. The uncivilized believe that pretending to be civilized will make these activities less supernatural, which highlights the obvious that the uncivilized are severely mentally impaired of intelligence for lawful social functioning.

There are very serious restrictions on the uncivilized being able to have personal contact with the civilized because of the harmful effects of direct or indirect supernaturalism on the civil constitution whether they pretend to be civilized or not. This means that they cannot then establish a relationship with the civilized through the thing that restricts personal contact or relationship with the civilized, supernaturalism.

Acts against humanity are serious crimes in international law, the civil constitution is recognized as a human being , so when the uncivilized misuse their supernatural powers and senses to harm the civilized mentally or physically or violate the civil rights of the civilized, those actions are the real acts against humanity.

Supernatural political dramatics feed off insecurities, fear or anxiety, discrediting the vulnerable because it is a very unlawful practice. Unfortunately for the uncivilized the perfect test subjects for these political supernatural dramatics the civilized or the law cannot be involved in it as it represents lawlessness which defeats the purpose of the creation of the law. They have an impossible task discrediting the law or the civilized.

Real acts against humanity or crimes against humanity are the misuse of supernatural powers and senses by the uncivilized to harm mentally or physically the civilized or to violate the civil rights of the civilized. These acts include the indirect misuse of supernatural powers and senses by the uncivilized pretending to be civilized. Acts or crimes against humanity are taken very seriously in international law. International law only recognizes the civil constitution as human being for the purposes of protection against crimes against humanity. Given the political nature of the uncivilized constitution and not being recognized by both domestic and international laws, which means under the doctrine of a jury of your peers they cannot sit in judgement or judge the civilized constitution. This is because it is implied that their judgement will be impaired. So in circumstances under domestic or international laws requiring a degree of judgement the uncivilized should consider requests or communications from the legally recognized constitution, the civil constitution, as commands or instructions or orders. To try to judge the civil constitution will be interpreted as a crime against humanity.

Politics or the uncivilized political constitution represents lawlessness and cannot be allowed to manipulate the law or the civilized legal constitution to create an outcome they prefer because that would lead to the creation of hell on earth. It is similar to allowing prisoners to create prison rules instead of the government which will defeat the rehabilitation objective. To try to manipulate, alter the civil constitution supernaturally for this purpose is a crime against humanity.

It has been established that the differences between the civilized and the uncivilized constitutions mean that the civilized are morally infallible; the civilized are incapable of sinning or committing crimes. When the uncivilized misuse their supernatural powers and senses to create false impressions that the civilized are capable of sinning or committing crimes in order to undermine law and order, they are acts or crimes against humanity.

The civilized or the law deals with a situation in a straightforward clear way and the uncivilized or lawlessness deals with a situation in a bent confusing way, the uncivilized have the tendency to want to drag things on for a long time preferably without any resolution which caters to their hyperactive supernatural nature at the expense of the mental and physical wellbeing of the vulnerable and law and order.

The law, the bible, does not accept apologies or forgive a supernatural or the uncivilized when they misuse their supernatural powers and senses to harm the civilized mentally or physically or to breach the peace in a civilized society because it has correctly determined that any attacks on the civilized or in a civilized society by a supernatural has been deliberately calculated as a consequence of their supernatural powers and senses.

Matters of law and order cannot be left to a lawless uncivilized political constitution as confirmed by the bible because they will always make compromises to cater to their uncivilized constitutions rather than make decisions in the interest of peace and security, law and order. It is strange that for those that are obsessed with masculinity both the males and females of the uncivilized constitutions they are extremely weak on real issues that are a measure of real strength.

The natural weakness of the uncivilized constitution forces them to unlawfully attempt to establish or create supernatural relationships with the civilized when they cannot create normal civilized relationships, which is beyond the natural capabilities of the civilized constitution. They try to create these unlawful supernatural relationships with the civilized for the purposes of treachery to undermine law and order and the constitutional role of the civilized as law lords.

The laws, both domestic and international laws are very strict on the confirmation of the existence of a relationship between individuals even when they believe the individuals to be of the civilized constitution for law and order purposes. Some of these relationships include marriages, contracts for goods and services etcetera. You will need to provide documentary evidence to prove the existence of these relationships. In circumstances where there is no documentary evidence the individuals concerned will be required to prove its existence within the realm of what is possible under the law. The main element in any of these relationships is consent under the law. This requirement is meant to eliminate problems like rape, theft, and kidnapping or abduction etcetera. So when a supernatural tries to create a supernatural relationship with the civilized beyond the natural capabilities of the civil constitution to enter into or consent to, it will be interpreted as an act or crime against humanity.

The psychological profile of those that rape, paedophiles, and sexual harassment at work, the offenders usually make the lives of their victims hell when their unlawful advances are rejected. Promotions, benefits etcetera if the offender is in a position of power, are not dependent on merit but on the rejection of the unlawful advances. These are constant experiences of the civilized when the unlawful unhealthy practices of the uncivilized are correctly rejected or an illegitimate supernatural government is rejected. The uncivilized collectively have the characteristics of rapists and paedophiles.

Victors in a war or armed conflict or countries that unlawfully invade other countries always rewrite history to make their actions seem right or honourable. Unfortunately I am sure that this is what has happened to history's portrayal of Lord Adam by the uncivilized.

It is convenient for the uncivilized to direct their attention to the symptoms of a problem rather than the cause because they will be identified as the culprits and it keeps the problem unresolved indefinitely which suits their hyperactive supernatural constitution. There is a difference between being aware of the existence of the differences between the civilized and the uncivilized constitutions because it has been revealed to you and being aware of it because you are supernatural.

The constitution, the bible, has made a determination that the uncivilized are wicked and as a consequence condemned. Can the condemned the uncivilized be a jury of the peers of the righteous the civilized? Absolutely not, the uncivilized are not in the same peer group as the civilized. From my observations life is impossible for the supernatural constitution and to feel they need to create hostile living conditions, which means condemn themselves to hell which is the opposite for the civilized constitution.

Domestic and international laws do not recognize the possibility of human beings being able to enter into a supernatural relation with a supernatural the same way the laws have made a determination that a minor cannot consent to having sex with an adult. So when the uncivilized try to manipulate the lives of the civilized for their unlawful supernatural political dramatics beyond the natural capabilities of the civilized to enter into or consent to, it will be interpreted as acts or crimes against humanity.

When the uncivilized keep experiencing allergic reactions from the civilized constitution when they want to force unlawful indirect or direct contact with the civilized as if accident prone, it is because the civilized are naturally righteous with an in built defence mechanism against lawlessness. The rejection manifests as an illness, it then becomes an act or a crime against humanity to continue to force these unlawful contacts. This also applies when they misuse their supernatural powers and senses to create false impressions that the unlawful contact is voluntary.

Lord Adam as ruler was entitled to protection from harm as part of his sacred civil rights, including protection from persecution as a result of prejudices as a consequence of the differences between the civilized and the uncivilized constitutions. He had no supernatural powers and senses prior to the incident, so there was no criminal intent. His civil constitution could only have been altered supernaturally by a supernatural. As a juror of his peer group I must conclude that he was not guilty of any disobedience or crimes in the Garden of Eden.

2. A blame the victim culture by the uncivilized

These prejudices that lead to the unlawful persecution of the civilized by the uncivilized in some cases are as a result of bad judgement associated with the supernatural instinct of the uncivilized constitution with regard to the likes and dislikes of the civilized constitution. When things go wrong as a consequence of these bad judgements they blame the victims, the civilized.

There were compromises reached regarding the practice of politics, some groups were protected from political supernatural lawless dramatics. These groups were the monarchy, the civil service, the police force etcetera. Unfortunately these political supernatural lawless dramatics have extended to these protected groups. This is the problem with compromising with a sacred creation the law. The law never surrenders to lawlessness; compromises are not compatible with the proper operation of the law.

Both domestic and international laws do not recognize the supernatural constitution for purposes of playing games, joking or socializing with the civilized constitution. They consider it naturally impossible for the civil and supernatural constitutions to be compatible for such activities. I believe it ways of making the supernatural constitution take the constitutional role of the civil constitution as law lords very seriously.

To prove criminal intent when a crime has been committed, the person or persons must have supernatural powers and senses. A crime is defined by the real constitution, the bible, as the misuse of supernatural powers and senses to harm mentally or physically the civilized, the uncivilized or to breach the peace in a civilized society. The uncivilized are protected from crime under the real constitution when the official role of the civilized as law lords is acknowledged officially with its constitutional rights and privileges.

Crimes or acts against humanity are very serious crimes and it is taken very seriously because of its destabilizing effects on the security of the planet. Humanity is the law in the form of the civil constitution or human beings.

As a consequence of the gravity of the offence, acts or crimes against

humanity, there are no time limits regarding the prosecution of offenders.
The civil constitution is official or formal by nature as a living representation of the law, the uncivilized can only operate officially or legally by being commissioned by the law. It is as a consequence impossible for the law to commission supernatural lawless political activities.
Lord Adam's civil rights were initially unlawfully unnecessarily violated when he was interfered with to create Eve without his consent.
Crimes or acts against humanity are regarded as abominations, despicable actions and offenders must be severely punished. The Rome statute of international criminal court explanatory memorandum defines crimes against humanity as particularly odious offences in that they constitute a serious attack on human dignity or grave humiliation or a degradation of human beings.
Whether you are out and about or in the privacy of your home or watching a film or listening to music or reading a novel you are always under constant attacks from the uncivilized with their supernatural lawless political dramatics.
It is my understanding that the civilized and the uncivilized are created the same way and by natural selection the civilized are rulers. According to the real constitution, the uncivilized are meant to suffer severely and indiscriminately destroyed until a proper lawful system of government is in place headed by the civilized. Contrary to the deliberate misinterpretations of the bible by the uncivilized the civilized should not be harmed, the civilized are the victims and should not be blamed for the wickedness of the uncivilized pretending to be civilized.
It is quite unsettling for the civilized to be aware of the extremely dangerous nature of the uncivilized and to know that they are so hostile and initiate or instigate unprovoked attacks on the vulnerable and what stops them are only threats of retaliations and not good conscience.
The real constitution, the bible and domestic and international laws

only protects the civilized because a determination has been made that the existence of the differences between the civil and supernatural constitutions mean that the civil constitution is incapable of wrongdoing(sins and crimes).

The uncivilized behave like heroin addicts that constantly exploit the needs of the vulnerable for their harmful lawless supernatural political dramatics.

The uncivilized are not allowed contact, direct or indirect, with the civilized or to communicate directly or indirectly with the civilized under domestic or international laws because these laws do not recognize the supernatural constitution. The uncivilized interact with each other by acting or pretending, which is possible for the supernatural constitution because of their supernatural powers and senses but beyond the natural capabilities of the civil constitution because of the absence of supernatural powers and senses. The real constitution only allows limited contact with the civilized when the civil constitution is properly installed or recognized as law lords with its rights and privileges.

To force unlawful contact or communication with the civilized, or to force the civilized into role plays that are beyond the natural capabilities of the civil constitution, or to force contact or communication with the civilized under domestic and international laws while unlawfully pretending to be civilized are acts or crimes against humanity.

When the uncivilized conspire collectively to compromise the education or development of the civilized about human behaviour or practices including what are edible in order to undermine the constitutional role of the civilized as law lords are acts or crimes against humanity.

According to international law and the real constitution, acts or crimes against humanity are so serious that they are unforgivable.

Acts or crimes against humanity are the misuse of supernatural powers and senses by the uncivilized to harm the civilized mentally or physically or to breach the peace in a civilized society. These acts include making the civilized live our lives incomplete without our civil rights. The misuse of supernatural powers and senses to alter the civil constitution in order to undermine or compromise the constitutional role of the civil constitution as a law lord is an act or a crime against humanity.

Politics is an unlawful activity, it is a practice that allows people to join or vote for a political party, it is something or an activity suited to the supernatural political constitution. It is an activity or concept not suited to the civil legal constitution. The uncivilized can be swayed to join any political party because of their supernatural political constitution but not the civil legal constitution because it is beyond the natural capabilities of the civil legal constitution. The uncivilized cannot manipulate the civil constitution for their supernatural political activities because politics is a lawless activity that challenges the existence of the law and the civil constitution. The practice of politics is an act or crime against humanity. The political spectrum right wing blue and the left wing red are both political lawless supernatural practices that challenges or threatens the existence of the real constitution and the civil constitution. The political blue is a misrepresentation of true blue represented by the civil constitution, a supernatural sabotage.

The uncivilized like to create conditions that constantly give them something to do, which caters to their supernatural nature, at the expense of the mental and physical wellbeing of the civilized and the vulnerable. The law does not allow the uncivilized to put themselves between the civilized and what the civilized wants like goods and services etcetera. The replication technology in some of the science fiction films, trees with fruits, the bible suggest that it is possible to access goods and services etcetera in a civilized manner without the need for the uncivilized to get between the civilized and these goods and services. The law requires the uncivilized to provide goods and services as a one off, without the need for repairs and these goods and services must be able to self-replicate like trees and fruits. There is a difference between providing goods and services in a civilized manner to meet the needs of the civilized and the uncivilized unlawfully pretending to be civilized to provide these goods and services.

The uncivilized are in the habit of corrupting the development or education of the vulnerable and the civilized to get them used to a way of living only to enjoy the sadism or power trip of taking it away claiming moral justification, pot calling kettle black.

It is my constitutional role as a law lord to stop these supernatural sadistic practices.

When there is a lawful system of government in place then it will be only those amongst the uncivilized that commit crimes by misusing their supernatural powers and senses to harm the civilized, the uncivilized and breach the peace in a civilized society that will be punished. At the moment because of the lawless system of government, the constitution orders the indiscriminate destruction and continuous suffering of the uncivilized.

Under these circumstances, the lawless system of government, it is impossible for any supernatural whether pretending to be civilized or not to establish or claim to have a relationship with the law or the civil constitution. They are considered by the real constitution to be enemies of the law and the civil constitution.

The mannerisms, judgements, decisions or instincts of the supernatural are toxic to the civilized and in a civilized society. The uncivilized constitution is not compatible with the civilized constitution. The real constitution and the history of the nobility in the United Kingdom prohibit nobles or the civil constitution from socializing or having informal contact with the working class or the uncivilized. To try to force it is similar to making the civilized navigate around a minefield. The method of a solution to a problem by a supernatural is completely different to the civil constitution and will prove disruptive in a civilized society.

It appears that there are serious practical security reasons why the nobility requires ladies to go to a finishing school to learn how to behave properly in case they become companions of those that are really civilized. This will help minimize the intentional or unintentional compromise of the civil constitution similar to what Eve did to Lord Adam.

Once the uncivilized establish an unlawful delusional supernatural relationship with the civilized, beyond the natural capabilities of the civil constitution, they start supernaturally unlawfully toying with the civilized as if the civil constitution is an inanimate object or an animal in a zoo. They unlawfully supernaturally disrupt the plans of the civilized as if disrupting the plans of an animal in a zoo, whose plans they consider inferior or unimportant. These actions are acts or crimes against humanity.

The uncivilized have unlawfully altered the images in films and the voices in radio and music, the images and voices are now supernatural. The domestic and international laws do not allow these alterations when the civilized listen to radio or music or the civilized watch films or television. These alterations are unlawful and unhealthy and extremely hostile. When things go wrong as will inevitably be the case, they will always opt to blame the victims, the civilized. I have noticed that these unlawful alterations were tailored to interact directly or indirectly with me. I have no supernatural powers and senses to be able to have done these alterations myself because they were done supernaturally. I believe it to be a deliberate unlawful sabotage of my interests by the uncivilized for unlawful political purposes to try to undermine my civil rights. The intrusion on its own from the unlawful alterations is a violation of my right to privacy. The more outrageous the strange unlawful decision becomes the more they desperately try to misuse their supernatural powers and senses to undermine the credibility of their victim. Apart from the unhealthy effects of supernaturalism on the civil constitution, it is extremely boring. It is impossible to create a supernatural relationship with the civilized because it is beyond the natural capabilities of the civil constitution. These unlawful supernatural relationships forced on the civil constitution by the uncivilized will inevitably go wrong and they will conveniently blame the victims, the civilized.

ADAM

3. The ultimate miscarriage of justice

The price is always too high for the civil constitution when the uncivilized try to establish direct or indirect contact. The civilized are always taken on an unhealthy unlawful emotional rollercoaster ride by being unlawfully drawn into their unlawful supernatural dramatics, which are beyond the natural capabilities of the civil constitution. They enjoy toying with the emotions of those different from them especially the civilized. Animals with a reasonable amount of consciousness aware that they are being keep to be slaughtered for the consumption of the uncivilized. Animals watching as their children or parents are being slaughtered. There is a unique sadistic pattern of behaviour of the uncivilized constitution that is beyond the comprehension of the civil constitution. As a law lord I cannot stomach direct or indirect contact with the uncivilized. It is not going to get better. It has been getting worse and worse after becoming aware of the differences and the atrocities linked to supernatural powers and senses.

The uncivilized are naturally persecutory, discriminatory towards those different from them including the civilized. It is so bad that they are willing to misuse their supernatural powers and senses to create a false impression of wrongdoing to make the lives of the civilized revolve around constant abuse or torture with their supernatural powers and senses as punishment that caters to their sadistic nature. No law or laws will give a supernatural illegal political constitution legal authority over a civil legal constitution. They then rely on role play or acting which is governed by laws.

The supernatural constitution has the characteristics of a rapist and a paedophile; they rely heavily on unlawfully forcing themselves on those different from them.

The supernatural constitution is hostile by nature and on this basis they interact and establish relationships, which is not compatible with the civil constitution.

Their concept of heaven is based on their hostile constitution, the concept of a route to heaven and a place that is heaven is hostile and unlawful and a conspired attack on the civil constitution. It is a crime against humanity. The route is an embodiment of the unlawful violation of all the civil rights of the civil constitution.

When the uncivilized pretend to be civilized and advocate hostile living conditions as suitable for the civil constitution including the revised work concept, it is a crime against humanity.

The supernatural constitution, its nature and instinct are treacherous to the civil constitution and to a civilized society. There is always this overwhelming urge or tendency to cater to the lawless supernatural political constitution at the expense of peace and security.

Lord Adam never stood a chance. His development was dependent on a proper education without the alteration of his civil constitution.

The description of the supernatural constitution is a species or being or virus that is an immediate continuous threat to humanity and its existence. What does humanity do when faced with this type of threat? Humanity will try to get rid of it or destroy it.

Lord Adam by natural selection was confirmed as God and ruler, to undermine that is to undermine the existence of humanity.

The uncivilized because of their political nature like to claim responsibility for the installation of a king or ruler for power tripping purposes which contradicts the purpose of the law. If you are not legal you rely on influence or coercion.

Your skin colour, whether pink or brown, does not make you supernatural or civil, your constitution is determinant on whether you have supernatural powers and senses or not. Although Lord Adam has been depicted as pink skinned he was definitely made from brown mud or sand.

The civil constitution does not have to prove to anyone its morality, whether good or bad, the determination has been made that the civil constitution is good by nature, given the differences. It is the supernatural constitution that needs to prove its morality, whether they are good or bad. The civil constitution is good by nature and the supernatural constitution is good by actions.

Any extra demands put on the civil constitution regarding morality are beyond the natural capabilities of the civil constitution and are acts or crimes against humanity.

ADAM

4. Author's notes

ADAM

Adam is my ninth book about the law. It is the correct identification, interpretation and application of the laws of this planet. It reveals the purpose of the establishment of the United Nations, the international criminal court, and the identification of a serious crime referred to as acts or crimes against humanity. These acts or crimes against humanity are the misuse of supernatural powers and senses by the uncivilized with supernatural powers and senses to harm mentally or physically the civilized without supernatural powers and sense, and to breach the peace in a civilized society. It also reveals the conspiracy of the uncivilized to undermine law and order and the constitutional role of the civilized as law lords.

ADAM

5. Author's biography

ADAM

My name is Lord Loveday Ememe. I am a graduate of an Anglican seminary school. I am of a civilized constitution which makes me a law lord according to the real constitution of the United Kingdom, which is the Christian principles or the civil constitution of man. I also graduated from the University of East London with an honours degree in law.

ADAM

6. Bibliography

ADAM

The Bible
Wikipedia

www.ingramcontent.com/pod-product-compliance
Lightning Source LLC
Chambersburg PA
CBHW072306170526
45158CB00003BA/1208